SLEEPING KEYS

SLEEPING KEYS

Jean Sprackland

CAPE POETRY

Published by Jonathan Cape 2013

2 4 6 8 10 9 7 5 3 1

First published in Great Britain in 2013 by
Jonathan Cape
Random House, 20 Vauxhall Bridge Road,
London SW1V 2SA

www.randomhouse.co.uk

Addresses for companies within The Random House Group Limited can be found at:
www.randomhouse.co.uk/offices.htm

The Random House Group Limited Reg. No. 954009

A CIP catalogue record for this book is available from the British Library

ISBN 9780224097697

The Random House Group Limited supports the Forest Stewardship Council® (FSC®),
the leading international forest-certification organisation. Our books carrying the FSC label
are printed on FSC®-certified paper. FSC is the only forest-certification scheme
supported by the leading environmental organisations, including Greenpeace. Our paper
procurement policy can be found at www.randomhouse.co.uk/environment

MIX
Paper from
responsible sources
FSC® C016897

Typeset in Bembo by Palimpsest Book Production Limited
Falkirk, Stirlingshire

Printed and bound in Great Britain by
CPI Group (UK) Ltd, Croydon CR0 4YY

One feather, and the house, sinking, falling, would have turned and pitched downwards to the depths of darkness.

Virginia Woolf: *To the Lighthouse*

CONTENTS

SLEEPING KEYS

OPENING A CHIMNEY

lets in the world.
It was a stopped throat
but now voices travel through it:

the tremulous mantra of pigeons,
impetuous dogs
and the chatter of night trains.

Now the closed room is elemental.
Still air quivers with freshness.
The wind makes skittering incursions,

throws down hailstones
racketing into the grate
accurate as coins in a chute.

For years it was shut and intimate.
It forgot the outdoor sounds,
the smell of sky.

Now something falls, soft as a thought –
a clod of soot, or the bones of an old nest –
and the dreaming house stirs.

SHEPHERDESS AND SWAIN

Cremated bones go into china,
and it is too brittle you would think for these
come-hither folds of cloth with all their warm suggestions.

He has one knee on the blue-and-white ground
and the other pressed to her skirt.
He raises one badly painted eyebrow.
She urges him on from the corner of a smudged mouth.
His hand is on his racing heart,
she is reaching to touch his arm,
and the dew rises through them.

No, it is the wrong stuff: all gloss
and deadpan, suitable for vases and teapots.
There is dust in all its clefts and curlicues,
and tapped with a fingernail it makes a cold note.

This belongs on a mantelpiece in a dismal sitting room
where the chimney will not draw; where someone
bored with a lifetime of unheard melodies
would come in and pick it up

and look at the boy cross-eyed with lust
and the poor girl flushed and impatient,
the two of them trapped in this rictus of desire

and no release, no way to pitch the story on
except to knock them onto the hearth and smash them.

HOMEMAKING

How simple the act of slicing bread, how nourishing.
As I pare away the crust I think of
the scruffy old zoo, long since derelict,
in a town where I used to live.

As the money ran out, they installed a row of cages
each containing a loaf of bread and a family of mice.
You could see the mice at work in the tunnels,
eating the loaf hollow and sleeping in the chambers.

They ate their way in, and made it home.
They went on eating, and the structure
collapsed into crumbs around them.
The loaf was replaced, and the work began again.

For the keepers, it was easy:
they needed no guards or razor wire.
Stale loaves cost a few pence each,
and they would never run short of mice.

Here in the kitchen I stand with the knife in one hand
and the loaf in the other, remembering
that ruined street of bread houses,
their desperate smell under the high-watt bulbs.

WE COME BACK TO THIS

The square of lit glass over the door
damp course
title deeds

Where else to return but here
breathing this boxed-in air
standing at a window
or sluicing hands under the tap

What we call home amounts to
the ritual ways between rooms
stored warmth in the walls
the creak of the stair or the bed

You can stay up all night with a house
as with a lover
locked in tight
drunk on intimacy

The blue middle of the night
with the old songs playing
casts it as glamorous
unquittable

but in the brash six a.m.
and the first traffic sounds
you ache again
with the need to leave

imagining other spaces
undefiled
cool and milky with light
where you could be

        a simple figure in a white room
              with a plain table
a glass of water
                    a vase of apple blossom

                                        Or better still:
                          a house you will never enter
              nor haunt after your death
                          rooms full only of themselves

IT OCCURS TO MY MOTHER THAT SHE MIGHT BE DEAD

She's been stripping beds, gathering sheets for the wash,
a thing she's done each week since she was fifteen –
first during her mother's illness
then in all the houses of her married life –
grasping the sheets and heaping them on the landing,
stirring the air with crumbs and flakes of dust.

I tell her don't be silly of course she's not dead
and she says *But how would I know?*
I suggest she pinch herself, which I'm sure will settle it,
but she says *That's for dreaming, not dead.*
I don't think there's a test for dead. And turns
and goes on stacking dishes in the sink.

That must have been forty years ago. Now I wonder
whether my mother is still there, somewhere,
asking the same question. *How would I know?*
I remember the glint in her voice as she said it,
the icy terror that seized me. And now
I stand with my arms full of sheets, and suppose I'm alive.

THE AQUARIUM

They bought it second-hand from a woman who yawned
and smoked, scattering ash into the water.
The fish rose, thinking it was food.

Back home they set it up, that little theatre
with its lighting and silver bubble machine,
tropical backcloth, cave and pirate ship.

But it must have been out of true, and overnight
it settled by fractions in its metal frame.
Something would have to give. Meanwhile

the players made their entrances from behind
a curtain of weed, delivered their soliloquies.
They flirted. There was a chase, a duel scene.

She thought perhaps the glass had flexed a little,
tried to adapt, but the metal was too stiff
and right-angled. He said on the contrary

the frame had warped and the glass was too brittle.
Either way, it cracked like a pistol shot,
spilling its dramas. Anyone in the street

would have looked up and laughed to see them in that
box of light which resembled the box of water,
gesticulating like characters in a farce:

the boy distraught, his sister tousled and luminous
in her nightdress, dipping and scooping the net,
the parents baling like mad deckhands.

Tomorrow they would know the worst:
the ruined carpet, the marshy smell,
the brown seep through the bedroom ceiling,

but right now, every fish must be saved.
They would do this together. Ah! that's how they were
in those antediluvian days.

LETTER HOME

Gulls nest on the decks, and skunks in the cabins
of skiffs and cruisers scuttled by youths
with their penknives and tin-can fires.

What do I hope for, walking the dismal shingle?
The harbour is silt, and the people have lost
their names: shellback, fishwife, stevedore.

Take me back, o my country. I am shrunk in exile
and desiccating, where the rattle of sand
is like rat's feet under the marriage bed.

IN

First week in the new house, and a muddle over keys.
She's back from somewhere with her daughter in her arms,
three months old, electric with hunger.
It's dark and she can't raise her neighbour.

She rattles at the back door, tries to jemmy it
with a flat stone she finds in the garden,
unfastens a hairclip to pick the lock.
The baby's cries are loose wires jumping and sparking.

She walks to the phone box and calls the police,
who take a spade from the shed and hack down the door.
Such busting and splintering! Her own screams blaze up
and out through her daughter's mouth.

She hadn't reckoned on resistance. Happiness, then,
is not some delicate gift, but a locked and stubborn thing
you have to break open. Now for a sleepless night
of rain and wind before the making good.

HOUSEPLANTS

They lean together on the windowsills,
casting anorexic shadows,

they who were all lush foliage
and glamorous blooms, now

wasting the long days spinning cobwebs
and squandering their brown leaves.

Someone has left this place in a hurry.
Rain drums on the other side of the glass

and gushes from the broken gutter —
it's nothing but mirage.

The earth in their pots is dry as fossil
but the cactus still sets its trap of barbs.

OCTOBER

Skies, big skies, careening over in the wind;
great shoals of cloud pitching and jostling
in their rush to be anywhere other than here.

You hesitate on your doorstep, glance up
and something tugs in your chest, rips free like a leaf
and is sucked up and away. Everything's

finished here: raw-boned sycamores,
fields scalped and sodden. The houses are shut
and dustbins roll in their own filth in the street.

So you would take your chances, risk it all…
You stand for a moment with the keys in your hand
feeling the pull of the sky and the moment passing.

CCTV

Exalted on towers and posts and fitted with articulated necks
that tilt, cock and swivel like the necks of owls, silent and absolute.

Like owls, they have a zealous gaze that does not falter, through no
    matter
how long a night. Unlike owls they sometimes hunt in pairs or threes,

perched at the corner of a flat roof, protected in cages or bulletproof
    housing,
some with a mohican of spikes. Not gregarious – no, not that at
    all –

and for all their cutting-edge robotics, they are nothing without
    the database.
They are not gods but Recording Angels. They come not flaming,
    sheathed in light,

but just as dread: all actions witnessed at thirty frames per second,
compressed by algorithm, returned by co-ax cable.

Theirs is the platform and the underpass, the building site and the
    park gates,
the bridge, the bus stop, the school playground and the cash machine.

Theirs is the doorway where you hope for darkness to cover you;
theirs is the scar on your hand and the make of your watch and
    your eyes.

LETTER HOME

Threads of rain fall through parched light
and desiccate, fritter away to vapour.

By the time they touch the skylight
they're nothing but pocks of dust on the glass.

How easily our wealth is spent.
He said and I said and it was gone.

The earth ticks over with grit and beetles.
The yellow tree curls its leaves into fists.

DISCOVERY

There was a time – she thinks she remembers it –
when rain dripping from a gutter at night
didn't sound like clocks ticking. The world
was richer and simpler then, the raindrop fattening
till it could not contain itself. Or there would be

a dress on the wet grass, not a cipher for the body
but a *thing* made of silk and dew. Now the rain
is stuck with her as if with some hopeless romantic
who keeps on making it stand for this or that
marvellous thing but never sees it true.

That apple she took from the bowl and cut in half
has a name, and a green skin flushed with red.
No need to think of temptation, original sin, etc.
It's just an apple, and she would ask nothing of it
except for sweetness. She was adamant.

But she's always been careless with knives. And look at her now,
trapped in the same old drama, here in the kitchen,
under the cold striplight: the wet blade,
the welling blood, the apple halved and glistening.
Autumn, the quiet house, the marriage done.

CLEARING THE DRAIN

The only thing that will work, he tells her,
is the hot tap for one full minute a day.

How pure and extravagant it is,
steaming and gushing in the empty sink,

all going to waste. She pictures it,
the bright redemptive rush, knifing through

the clag and fur of decay, the mutating
slivers and scraps she's swilled and sluiced

down that silver throat, into the secret
vaults and passageways, where now

the clean water surges, blinding
and purging like white light.

TWO WINDOWS

When they fought for the last time
the bedroom window, slabbed with old glass,
stirred the familiar view into ripples,
the way a bonfire or a church candle
liquifies the air above.
Branches and telegraph wires
warped and snapped as she moved about the room,
the moon changed beyond its own logic.

Now she lives alone she notices
as she climbs the basement stairs
the corrugated pane in the front door
seeping with light from the bottom up,
like warmth spreading from cell to cell.
Close up, it's more random: a mass
of membranes, trembling like frogspawn,
trying to net the day, unable to hold it.

THE NEW ORDER

I sweep the bedroom clean
of all its careful little graven images.
But in the cupboard under the stairs

a donkey-jacket hangs and a football scarf.
Well, you can't tell a cupboard anything,
it's incapable of adapting. And then the shed,

full of the old language and customs:
tricycle, beach spade, piece of cracked felt
once meant for the roof. The news

has not reached here, and venerable spiders
keep the faith. As for the toolbox
and its fusewire, cup-hooks, spirit level –

obsolete from the start.
Tobacco tin, with your oily rattle:
you have two choices.

SLEEPING KEYS

Printed with old roses or tartan and thistle,
there's a biscuit tin like this in every house.
Prise off the lid and catch the flinty scent
of old keys, decommissioned and sleeping.

Like unspent francs, deutschmarks and drachmas
they accumulate here, inert and futureless,
though each in its time was powerful:
precision-cut on a wheel of sparks.

Tip them out on the table in the empty kitchen
and rake through them one last time.
The mortice for the first front door,
the yale for the porch, replaced ten years ago
(never a good copy, it balked at the turn).

These antiques were for internal doors,
this one perhaps the old bathroom where
he knocked softly, and you stepped out of the bath
and printed the bare boards with your feet
as you hurried to unlock and let him in.

Padlock keys for sheds and bikes, and a set
with a jaunty tag for the house next door, though
the people are different now and you can't imagine
popping round and watering the plants.

Count out their obsolete treasure on the table,
puzzling as your grandmother's brooches and hatpins
and with the same residual gravity –
the shiny, the worn, the ones threaded
on string or paperclips, or marked with Tipp-Ex,
the miniatures for medicine cabinets and pianos –

then scoop the lot into the bin, because
not one will ever spring a lock again
to let him into your space, or you to his.
No more the easy click of the blade engaging
and nudging the bolt aside, or his grin as he entered
the room of steam, already slipping off his shirt.

LETTER HOME

Sunlight patterns on the opposite wall
are like jewellery, trembling on a girl's wrist
as she turns it and admires it.

All day the wall of this borrowed room
is a screen for the vanities of light,

slipping hour by hour as the sun moves,
bleaching and dissolving when clouds cross it.

Then the jealous chill of evening
when the projector fails at last
and the girl's wrist is bare as bone.

AT NIGHT IN THE HOUSE

At night in the house
  a river runs through her

        carrying its burdens
the golden barges   the dead griefs and the quick fishes

                    She lies alone
              wet at the mouth
                    and between the legs

and it runs not always placid
      sometimes angry   rough as old rope

dragging its way
        between the receding banks
    the old wharves worn smooth
            by all the moorings made there

the scrolled barges
with their forgotten cargoes
of sugar   tobacco   raw silk

                  and the illicit little night boats
                  tied up swiftly
          while the moon was behind a cloud

              the twelve slithery steps
                cut into the dripping wall

When the river is running hard
    she speaks only its own tongue
              not the dry-docked language
              of other people

and in places
        the trees lean in
                    like conspirators
            and the water is smeared
        with whispers

                    and in places
                        the bank
                                melts into the water
                                    roots and all
                                    rocks and all
                        even an unlucky heifer
                        risking the edge for a drink

In the night house
        she is nothing but riverbanks
            all she can feel is river
                        drawn through her
                                like a green rope

                    scouring the banks
                                with restlessness
hauled
        towards open sea
                    taking its freight
                            of corpses
            and drowned silverware

LAST RESORT

i.m. Joyce Lockley, 1933–2011

i

Borneo, 1951. Deep in the interior,
on the deep jungle floor, a young missionary is kneeling

not in prayer, but in the equally experimental service
of edging a spatula into the earth
and collecting a few rich crumbs for the vial.

He has gone, as the letter said he should,
far from the beaten track. He has left the village
and walked for four hours to this small clearing

where the forest steams and swells around him
with the cries of mynah and hornbill, gibbon, cicada.

Sweat prickles his neck as he seals the vial.
A horned beetle, polished like a sideboard,
runs over his gloved hand. He's no scientist

but he knows the words of Ecclesiastes:
The Lord hath created medicines out of the earth;
and he that is wise will not abhor them.

In the lab back home in Indiana,
his friend the chemist will analyse

these gentle scrapings of soil and spoor,
isolate a new microbe, and name it 08565.

The lead-grey lift continues past our floor,
up to the very top, out of bounds to the public,
and in steps a man in a high-vis jacket
with a hawk standing on his gloved hand. A hawk
with bronze shoulders and hooked beak.

Twice a week they fly her at dusk, he tells me,
when the city's pigeons commute here for roosts.
She is at heart a huntress, but trained
in the ways of deterrence. Still, says her man
with pride, she does sometimes kill.

Into the airless lift where I stand like a dead thing,
she brings the scent of November, her feathers still damp
with the floodlit air where she circled just now
over the flat roofs, the chimneys and vents,
the maintenance routes and air ambulance landing pad:
all the great sprawling body of the hospital.

Into this shut-up place she comes heraldic,
in her wings the memory of thrust and soar,
of the sudden stoop and the canceleer
before he called her back to the glove to feed.
And I look and look into her unreadable eyes,
stung by a fierceness and freshness I thought was lost.

Two floors down, in a room as deep
and remote as the deep jungle clearing,
a new front has opened in the long microbial war

and that front is my mother.
On one side, bilateral pneumonia.
The old man's friend. The coup de grâce.

On the other, the antibiotic drip
delivering its metered dose of 08565:
the wonder drug, the drug of last resort.

Into the shut-up place of the body it comes
bringing the distant memory of soil and spoor:
Vancomycin. It has saved many lives

but here, in the battlefield of my mother's body,
infection blooms and swells
and will not be vanquished. I sit and look

into her unreadable eyes. Pegged to her finger
a small barometer shows the chances:
low, and falling. Even so

when this is over, a day or two from now,
and I'm counting through my hoard of petty regrets,
I'll wish I'd told her about the missionary.

A good man. Nothing in it for him –
just the walk and the heat, the letter in his pocket
and the restless, living earth where he knelt.

A thin blue curtain divides the world in two:
the dying from the living. On this low-lit side,
her breathing has become the measure of everything;
all human experience slips through the funnel of this sound.

All her days she has been open to breath,
but is closing now against its simple gifts.
Her lungs are drenched flat as the wings of the butterfly
I tried to rescue from the pool in summer.

On the other side of the curtain, the brilliant
clatter of instruments on a trolley, the slam
of a metal drawer on the nurses' station,
voices, a burst of laughter.

Who would have thought death could be present here,
in the same room as life? I mistook them for opposites.

She takes small sips of air as if it were unfamiliar
and she not sure she'll like it. Should I
pull the curtain aside and call out
this air doesn't work, can they bring her another kind?

THE BIRDS OF THE AIR

I'm vague about their names –

laziness, yes, but also a wish
to keep them free. Isn't it enough
to foul their brooks and fields
and flay the high trees with our floodlights

without this last assault of language?
I limit myself
to the one thing I know:
that they are *light*

(the word splits on a prism,
revealing them luminous, weightless
and all tones between).

I learnt this as a child
in the little yard behind the chapel
where I would be sent with the leftover bread.
When I stepped out from the cool, screened interior

they were waiting in the sunshine.
They glittered in the branches
while I crumbled the host and scattered it
among the weeds and broken paving.

DEATH'S HEAD HAWK MOTH

'It commits such extensive depredations on the honey of bee hives, that it has been by some denominated the bee-tiger.'

James Francis Stephens

By day it feeds quietly on potato and snowberry,
lays its eggs under the leaves of the nightshade,
flattens itself invisible on the bark of a tree;

but when it comes bluffing at the moonlit hive
the sign of the skull stamped on its thorax
should announce it clearly enough.

Ever since it settled on the scaffold at Whitehall
just as the king's head was held before the crowd
its ominous costume has struck a human nerve,

but here on the threshold of sweetness
it folds the dark cloak of its wings
which are no stronger than powdered gauze

and the bees hasten to give a royal welcome.
It has disguised itself with their special scent
and the shrill note it sings to soothe them.

How easy the doorstep swindle!
How eagerly the false queen is courted,
the treasure yielded up, the contract sealed.

LETTER HOME

In the library I search an atlas
but the towns have foreign names, and travel by water
seems unlikely — those shifting green geometries,
the glitter and surge and whalesong.

What recommended me to this place? How am I qualified?
Sometimes I smell snow, or petrol, very remote.
What shall I hope for, out on the hardfaced yard
and the steel corridors that flash and slam like jaws?

Each morning the librarian waits with a towel
to wipe us clean of other people's spit.
She the keeper of elsewheres, who still insists
on legends of navigation by starlight.

AUGUST JOURNEYS

Lammas

A farmhouse sunk in a sea of rye.
The neighbouring field scraped to stubble.

Haybales bulging at the barn door.
The empty shippon and the acre of black plastic.

Allotments of buckets and bolted lettuce.
Factory windows blacked out by sunlight.

Sky-blue render torn from the side of a house.
A digger broken-necked on the embankment.

The catch in the rook's voice.
A dismembered bicycle slung to a signpost.

The year brimming and ready to spill.
Trackside willowherb turning to ash.

Transfiguration

On the sunlit road by the wind farm
I watch the long limb of a turbine
throw down a blade of shadow
which scythes the cornfield over and over
with a sudden rumour of night

Late Summer Holiday

The city lies open to me:
its garden squares, fountains and galleries.
I walk in, and no one checks my documents.

There are no keys to the city.
On quiet streets, I sit and breathe
where orange trees make scented shade

and oranges rot on the cobbles.
I think of nothing. The river is streaked
with the tolerant colours of sky.

THIRST

Come in from the sun:
from the clenched fist of noon
and the dazzle of scree

where the adder rustles the grey scrub
and the skirl of crickets
draws the air tense like wires.

Follow the path under the trees
blinded a moment by shadow
crushing wild marjoram underfoot

and you meet a small stone Virgin
her face blotched with lichen
and the sorrow of centuries.

Beneath, cool water leaks
from the body of the cliff
and is lost in the earth crevices.

It runs with the smallest of sounds
like the Virgin herself
running her tongue over her own dry lips

as consolation in the wait of ages.
And where the single film of water
slides over the green stone

the wasps approach, scores of them,
hovering close enough to taste
the invisible mist which must rise there.

Here the despised and the profane
whose golden bodies seem to be
fashioned from the heat of this day

hold their secret congregations
touching the shrine with fire
in return for moisture

their quick wings thrumming
as they come into her presence
and sip at her feet.

might be considered cousins
for their cracked and dirty whiteness,

their rough otherworldliness
and evasive mention of light,

their likewise capacity
to stop decay and guard wholesomeness.

Pressed to a wound, each draws
its own draught of pain:

one deep and amnesiac
the other urgent and merciless.

So haul me aboard, haul me in
and pack me in salt and ice –

each hurts in its own way;
each in its own way heals.

FOOTINGS

Spring, and the tang of fresh concrete in the air.
Someone has decided to stay, and they've dug the footings.
They staked and measured, cut a trench and scooped it out.
It's like making a grave, and there are often bones

but they don't matter – it's the clunk of a sewer,
the shock of cable the workmen dread. Still
we must all be anchored somehow, so they dug down
below the frostline, poured the readymix
and let the soil and bedrock bear the weight.

Earth's holdings are mud, and all our buildings
are straws drawing up water. In time
black mould will bloom on the plaster,
floorboards will rot, brickwork split.
Even the aggregate will crumble, all its constituents
seep back to their sources – limestone, sand, fly ash, gypsum –
whatever was mixed drain away into separateness.

But let's not grieve for our fallen houses.
We're through with one winter, and the next
is only a rumour. This is a time for building.
The wet screed shines. I can hear birdsong.

LETTER HOME

On the fells above town
it's still winter.

The high ridge bristles with rocks;
a bird's cry swings open like a rusty gate.

The way is strewn with toppled statues:
everywhere signs of the old regime.

An iced cobweb
has its own cosmology

and the fretworked pond is like
the fancy glass of a suburban porch.

I kneel and stare (o my country)
but the hall beyond is private and obscure.

What can I hope for in this lonely place?
I must kneel on the stones and wait

until the ash gives up its keys
and the track runs brown with thaw.

THE COVENANT

This grey morning carries
the promise of subtle music:
rain sleeking cast iron
and running safely to ground.

Yesterday I climbed an extending ladder
bringing tools on a red canvas belt
and tended to my gutters.
I checked them for rust,
learning their structure, naming the parts:
swan neck, hopper head, anglepiece, shoe.
I screwed the eared sockets tight to the walls.
I tugged whipcords of ivy
from its rooting places in the brickwork,
hooked out the martins' nest
and tossed it down –
it splintered on the path.

I live alone now, and things are simple.
This is the covenant:
I keep the ladder ready behind the shed,
and the storm is earthed.

LEAP DAY

Day of conditionals,
even the wind doesn't know you.

Weatherless day,
suspended between
before and after.

Steel chairs outside the café
reflect an egg-white sky

and I sit neither grieving
nor beyond grief.

The park hesitates between
graveyard and carnival –

birdsong welling up
through gaps in the traffic noise,

a blur of early blossom
among the sapless frames
of trees and memorial benches:

Arthur, till we meet again,
Laurie, who loved this place.

Day of amnesty,
first anniversary of nothing.

Children with clipboards
walk what's left of the avenue of elms
with its vista of hoardings and new-build

and they are digging up Green Lanes again
installing broadband cables
among the bits of bone and drover's rag.

Day of shadows:
Not just the losses of the past,
which are always with us,

but the spectral futures
we will have to stride the ditch to reach.

MOVING THE PIANO

It was damp in its joints, hamstrung and hipshot.
It still had a grubby mouthful of elephant.
The casewood hankered
after the big trees of the empire.

It was all stubborn resistance,
groaning and slubbering, innards jangling.
Something broke loose with a clunk.
We balanced the lid on its weak hinges

but the thing had slipped deep
into the interstitial dark.
The frame looked quaint as a spinning jenny.
It stank of old felt and lamentations.

It would take two strong men
and a third to watch the doorposts.
It would take a dolly, a humpstrap and two blankets.
There would be cursing at the turn of the stairs

and it would be a dead weight, passive as an invalid,
knowing its time has gone, but wanting only
to be left alone in its own home,
in its own wavering patch of light

while the clamorous room fades
to a tinnitus of dust and dead wasps.

TAKING DOWN THE SCAFFOLDING

Two stuntmen on a forty-foot tower.
One loosens the couplers, unclips the pulleys,
feeds through a gap above his head
a pole long as the house, for his mate
to lower over the roof edge –
it catches and he rocks it clanging free.

An hour later, they're nearly done.
The ladders and decks are chucked and stashed,
the apprentice checks them off and stacks the trailer.
And now to the blue plastic sheeting which has
snapped and billowed through so many windy nights –
they roll it thunderously and drop it through.

They know the risks, how much they can subtract
without collapse. They work together,
checking the angles, testing and sharing the weight.
They sing and banter, though one slip
could kill them both. What love you need
to dismantle the structure you're standing on!

THE FUSEBOX

I came here at times of crisis,
fumbling for the camping torch
which cast a simple disc of light
on the row of coded snibs,
the swags of cable gone stiff with age.

I would part the musty curtain of coats,
examine the panel with its dim legends
to the maps of circuitry walled up in this house:
eighty years of cutting, joining, routing and re-routing
which sparked the place to life, fired it with jazz and industry,
spun the meter wheel and ran this whole machine.

Today I have walked the echoing hall
and come to kneel here for the last time
in the buzzing dark of the cupboard
with its lost smell of rubber and bakelite.
By thinning torchlight I contemplate
the sequence of decisions, each of them binary,

and the black lever, whose heavy syllable
will override them all.

LETTER HOME

The little copse,
thick with birdsong yesterday,
is blasted bare.

I am guarding barbed wire
and a punctured water can.
My rifle is jammed with mud.

Take me back.
I am lost in exile, I am landlocked.
Guide me under the guns

to my own shore
where rain has a different sound:
water touching water,

the ecstatic meeting
of like with like,
itself a homecoming.

GOING BACK

'The thing itself always escapes'
Jacques Derrida

All I remember is pegging white sheets to the line,
planting tomatoes, kindling a fire in the hearth.
I was paler than now. I see myself drifting
through vague changes of season, a child in my arms
or something to stir on the stove.

Further back: the girl walking home at night
down the middle of the road to avoid dark gateways.
There was always a moon, and the sound of cattle
breathing by the hedge, and I was always alone,
carrying my bad shoes and thinking unreadable thoughts.

Now I climb the steps to the porch where the robin nested,
hoping to hear a scrap of my old voice. Hard to say
whether I'm singing or weeping. This doorknob often
caught my sleeve and yanked me back,
but I can never catch hold of my past selves like that –

I'm always a ghost to myself, except precisely *here*
in a present so thin it can scarcely be said to exist:
moment chases moment, so close they almost touch
and from that flickering succession I improvise
substance, continuity, survival.

I take down a book from my shelf,
draw the curtains, feel texture and gist,
but the fabric is nothing but threads, and all this
is straggling away even now
into the dim-lit past. Will I come back one day

and ask my own blank face at the window
what happened here? The moon
still hangs above that road, but the cattle have gone.
If I lean towards the future, I can already see myself
blown like spores over the hedges and fields.

SUPRA-VENTRICULAR TACHYCARDIA

Shocking to learn the heart's element is not love
but electricity. It's bathed in signals.
The wet circuits spark, the armature vibrates.

A beautiful piece of wiring the syncytium:
all the cells of the heart connected by bridges,
and the electric shiver sprinting across.

But my excitable cells don't wait for the messenger.
They jump at rumour and guesswork. So the trip
and thud, the voltage spike –

and all I can do is stop and wait
and listen to the fibrillation,
my own system arcing and shorting.

This heart is what I carry. It's what carries me.
This twitching fist of gristle, this hurt machine,
this rigged ship in a bottle.

AUBERGINE

No surprise they thought it poisonous,
with that seductive shine –
it has a night shade, and is of nightshade stock.
Cousin to tobacco, too solid for smoke,
still it might be believed a kind of stimulant.

A knife meets resistance –
like human skin, it gives and springs back,
buying time for the knife to think twice.
Inside, incongruous flesh dry as sponge,
a greenish catacomb for pale oblivious seeds.

Air stains it, and salt draws bitter secretions
from a hidden gland. But spooned from the pot,
dripping and dark as meat, at a candlelit table
where we ate together that first evening,
it was transfigured:

rich and apocryphal like the wine at Cana.
The flame steadied, the shadows softened around us.

SEA HOLLY

When I came to live with him, I came bringing flowers.
Not the usual pale translucent blooms
with the rot already in them — neither he nor I
needed telling that love is fragile.

The flowers I chose were fierce and electric.
Where I come from, they thrust up through sand.
Spring tides and salt winds blitz them
but they blaze in the storm like blue torches.

On warm days, painted ladies glut on their nectar
and the candied root was once an aphrodisiac,
but the head of sweetness wears a steel collar,
a star of bracts sharp enough to draw blood.

I stood in the street, spiked with all my warnings.
And he opened the door, and the flowers and I went in.

GRACE AT CHRISTMAS

Not only for the way the whisky
flames in the glass and thaws the blood;
not only for the rattle of hailstones
down the chimney and doused by fire;
not just for the way the brand-new ring,
slipped cool on a finger, flushes with life;
or the warmth of the bed, and the warmth of another,
when streetlamps are spinning snow outside.

But also for the good, true cold,
shocking us back to all our senses:
the broken-off star of ice in the hand,
the sting of the wind and the quickening heart.
For the splintering light, and the frost in our voices,
striking, and making the strung air ring;
December cold with its wilder gifts –
for when are we more alive than now?

UP

It's the staircases I remember:
the optimistic reach of them,
the erotic promise —

for who has not waited breathlessly
with curtains drawn against the afternoon
for the sound of a lover taking the stairs two at a time,

or hurried upwards together, shedding clothes,
and failed to make it to the top?
Then that other intimacy:

the naked foot
testing outside the walkline,
knowing the creak of the tread, and the giveaway.

When a house is built, this is a moment of vision:
the installation of the staircase.
A grand sweep of ambition, bridging the gap,

linking the two worlds: public with private,
utility with pleasure. Preparing the way
for the traffic of desire.

Where I am now, I climb and climb —
this new love is a tall place to live.
The staircase itself draws me on

away from the domestic spaces,
past the throb of the washing machine,
the landing with its case of forgotten thrillers,

past the loft, the quiet music
of the water tank, time expanding
in the copper pipes, the slow

curl of photographs in an old suitcase.
Up and up, as if I could climb forever,
as if gravity might let me go –

the risen heat, and the sun at the skylight
dazzling me into
a sudden forgetting of self.

ACKNOWLEDGEMENTS

Acknowledgements are due to the following publications:

Antiphon, Guardian, London Review of Books, Manhattan Review, Poem, Poetry Review, The North, The Reader.

Some of these poems have been broadcast on BBC Radio 4.